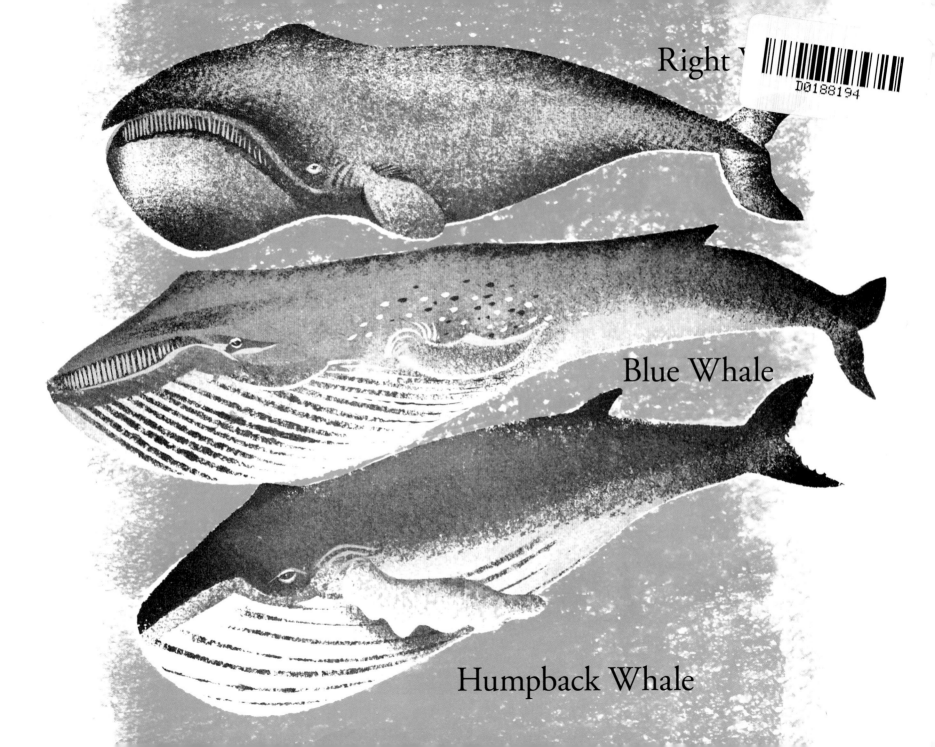

Right W

Blue Whale

Humpback Whale

First published in 1965 by Doubleday & Company, Inc., New York

Text © Johanna Johnston, 1965. Illustrations © Leonard Weisgard, 1965. All rights reserved

Reissued in 2015 by the Bodleian Library, Broad Street, Oxford OX1 3BG

www.bodleianshop.co.uk ISBN: 978 1 85124 428 7

Text © The Estate of Johanna Johnston, 2015. Illustrations © The Estate of Leonard Weisgard, 2015. All rights reserved

Printed and bound on FSC paper by Toppan, China.

Whale's Way

Johanna Johnston

Illustrated by Leonard Weisgard

Bodleian Children's Books

WHO has seen a whale?

Who has seen that giant creature leap out of the water, turn in the air, hit the water with his tail, then dive from sight again? Not many people—for the whale's way is a way that lies far from the ways of man.

The oceans curl all around the world. And up near the North Pole, down near the South Pole, are oceans that few people travel. When summer comes to those oceans around the poles, whales are there. Blue whales, grey whales, finbacks—all of them swim in those far, cold seas.

Humpback whales are there too. They are not the biggest whales. The blue whales are much bigger—the largest creatures alive. Compared to blue whales, humpbacks are only middle-sized. Even so, each humpback weighs five times as much as an elephant. And that is not small.

Like all the other whales in the polar seas, the humpbacks are
there to feast. They are feeding on a delicate food that floats
in the water there like a blanket—green or red or yellow. It
is made up of tiny shrimp and the smallest kind of plants, all
mixed together. The mixture is called plankton, a word that
means drifting.

The whales move along beneath the surface of the ocean, their
great mouths open to take in the plankton.

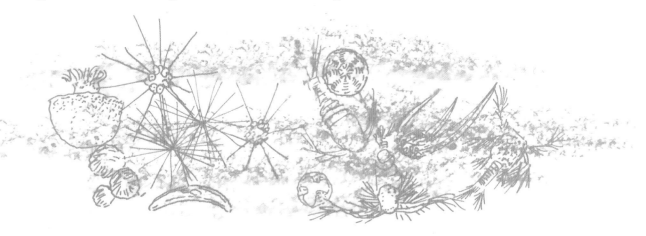

Some whales have teeth. They do not eat plankton. But the humpbacks, the blue whales, the finbacks and the greys do not have teeth. Instead, they have a sort of curtain in their mouths. It is baleen—long, thin, bony slats that hang in close rows from the roofs of their mouths to the bottoms. This curtain of baleen makes plankton just the right food for them.

The humpback and all the other baleen whales glide along under the water. Water and plankton pour into their mouths. Then they close their mouths and push up their huge tongues. The plankton rushes through the curtain of baleen. The water goes out into the ocean again.

Gliding along, gulping in plankton, the humpbacks graze through the water like cows in a meadow.

Every five or ten minutes, humpback whales rise to the surface to breathe. All whales breathe air, just like creatures that live on land. There are two blowholes in the top of each humpback's head. When a humpback rises to breathe, he blows his breath out through these blowholes. Two jets of vapour rise into the air. The sea is dotted with jets that look like fountains when many whales rise to breathe at once.

After breathing out, the whales breathe in, to fill their lungs with fresh air. Then down they go again, to graze once more.

But gradually summer comes to an end. There is more and more ice in the water. There is snow in the air.

When winter comes to one of the poles, it is summer at the other. But at the middle of the world, all along that middle belt called the Equator, it is summer the whole year round.

And so, when winter comes to a polar sea, the whales that are there head towards the Equator, where the water is always warm.

Off they swim, towards the middle of the world.

Their tails—called flukes—are broad and flat, very different from fishes' tails. For whales are not fish, but warm-blooded animals. Moving their flukes up and down and twisting them around, the whales scull themselves through the water. Every so often they must rise to breathe. Then they dive down and swim on.

A hundred miles, two hundred miles, five hundred miles— what are such distances to the whales? The ocean is their lake.

A thousand miles, two thousand miles they swim. At last they come to the place where the seas are warm and clear.

The humpbacks have travelled a quarter of the way around the world to find this warm sea. They rise and blow out their breaths in high jets of vapour. They breathe in deeply. Then they begin to play.

No other whales play quite as the humpbacks do. One of them dives and then swims up, up, until he leaps free of the water completely. The spray of the water showers around him. He turns in the air and flips his flukes high. Then he comes down onto the water and whacks it with his flukes. The sound is like the explosion of a cannon.

Another joins the game. Then another. Soon many humpbacks are playing, scattered across their ocean playground. They leap. They turn. They crash against the water, clapping it with their flukes. Now the sound is like the thunder of a dozen cannons.

After the first flurry, they rest a while. Then they begin to move in pairs, two by two. The humpbacks are choosing mates.

Two by two, they dive into the sea. Two by two, they swim around and about, playing tag, turning somersaults, slapping each other with their fins.

Grown humpbacks weigh thirty tons or more. But they leap and play as though that were nothing. And big as they are, they feel no need for food now. They do not eat at all during this time of play.

Days go by. Weeks go by. Then, at last, the time of playing and mating and fasting is over. The whales are ready to swim back the thousands of miles to the cold water near the pole.

Summer has come back to the polar sea when they reach it. The plankton is floating across the water again, an endless picnic.

The blue whales, the grey whales, the finbacks are returning too, after their months in warmer waters. All of them swim into the meadows of plankton and begin to graze.

Day after day they graze and glide, graze and glide. Until, once again, another polar summer has passed. Once again the snow and ice come, and it is time to leave for warmer waters.

Will it all be just as it was the year before—the long miles of travelling, then the months of play? Not for all the humpbacks.

Not all of them were playing last year, either. The warm waters near the middle of the world are more than a playground for the whales. The whales use those waters as a nursery too.

Some whales had their babies there last year. Now some of the humpbacks who played last year do not join the game. Their babies are being born.

How big is a baby whale?

Newly born, a baby humpback is almost as big as a full-grown elephant. But he is small beside his mother, and she nurses him just as mother cats do their kittens, just as mother cows nurse their calves. The baby humpback is a little calf too, a whale calf. Even when he is not nursing, he stays very close to his mother, near one of her fins.

The father whales, the bulls, play in the water, making the same great dives and leaps as they did a year ago.

But the cows and their calves are rocked gently in the cradle of the water. Every few minutes they rise to the surface to breathe. Then they coast down again.

Every day the calves grow bigger. But they are still very young when it is time to swim back to the polar sea. It will be a long journey for them.

Each mother swims close to her calf to protect him. Often the father whale swims on the other side of the calf.

A storm sweeps over the ocean. The father and mother guide their calf far below the surface of the water, where there is no hint of the storm above. Still, storm or no storm, they must rise to breathe.

Soon the storm is over. And when the whales rise, the sun is shining on the sea. It shines on the mist of their jets, making rainbows.

The father whale makes a great dive. Then he rushes up through the water to leap in the air. His dive and leap take him away from the mother and calf. Then, when he dives into the water again, he senses that danger is near.

How does he sense it?

His eyes are tiny and set one on either side of his great head. He cannot see far, either in or out of the water. It is through hearing that he learns the most. Now he senses that a pack of killer whales is nearby.

Killer whales are much smaller than he is. But they have teeth—strong, pointed teeth—and they feed on the flesh of other creatures. All other whales, even the biggest, fear the killers. All the creatures of the sea fear them, for the killer whales are the wolves of the ocean, fierce and cunning.

The mother whale is swimming off in terror, her calf huddled beside her. The father whale is terrified too. Frightening sounds come through the water. The killers have caught up with a whale swimming alone. They are attacking the lone whale, who is threshing about in fear and pain. The killers cluster around him, snapping and biting.

The father, the mother, the calf rush through the water—away, away. Big as they are, if the killers should follow them and catch them, they would be as helpless as the lone whale.

At last they feel safe enough to rise, take deep breaths, and then swim on more slowly.

Their eyes are so small and their sight is so poor that they do not realize another danger is not far away.

The danger is a black shape on the horizon. If the shape were nearer, the humpbacks might swim closer, trying to find out what it is. Humpbacks are curious and friendly.

The shape is a ship. Aboard it are men who are hunting whales. If they see a whale, they shoot at it with a harpoon that has a small bomb attached to its point. Long lengths of rope lead from the harpoon back to the ship. If a whale is struck by this harpoon, he can twist and turn, dive deep, leap high, swim as fast as he can, but it is almost impossible to get free.

The men on this ship do not see the mother and father whale and the calf, rising to spout their jets.

And so the mother, the father and the calf swim on. They have escaped the two greatest dangers that whales know—men, the hunters, and killer whales, their own relatives.

And now, at last, they come to the polar sea where the plankton drifts.

The mother and father whales open their mouths to gulp in the food. The calf, who has known nothing but his mother's milk so far, opens his mouth too.

The plankton streams into his mouth. He does not need any lessons. He closes his mouth and pushes with his tongue. The plankton streams through the baleen in his mouth. The water gushes out.

Now the calf is feeding himself.

How strange that such a delicate food should nourish a creature so big.

And how curious that even though the whale breathes air, he can never live on land. He must stay in the water—and still have air too. For if he could not come up regularly to breathe, spouting his jet, he would drown.

So the whale travels from ocean to ocean, now on the surface and now below—feasting, fasting, swimming, spouting and sometimes playing too. For that is the way of the largest creature on earth—that is the whale's way.

Finback Whale

Sperm Whale

Killer Whale